The Classical Unschooler: Education Without School

- Purva Brown -

This book is dedicated to homeschooling families. You are all amazing.

Table of Contents

Introduction	11
What is Classical Education?	15
- The Trivium	20
- The Grammar Stage	23
- The Logic Stage	27
- The Rhetoric Stage	31
- Mastery	33
What is Unschooling?	37
- The History of Unschooling	41
- What Unschooling is Not	43
- Some Current Unschooling Writers	47
Enter Classical Unschooling	49
The Five Tools of Classical Unschooling	53
- Strewing	55
- Conversations	59
- Memorization	61
- Interest-Led Learning	65
- Skills Learning	69
- Why?	71
Classical Unschooling in Action	73
Individual Subjects in Classical Unschooling	79
- Language Arts	83
- Math	93
- Science	101

- History 109
- Geography 117
- Other languages 123
- Music 125

Education is a Conversation, Not a Performance . . 127

Updates along the Journey 131

Acknowledgments 133

Introduction

"What happened to you?" a friend asked me late one night. The conversation had just shifted to how homeschooling was going. I had been bellyaching - I think - about moving from single digit to double digit subtraction and the ensuing drama (from my children) around it when her question cut through the banter. *What happened to you?*

"What do you mean?" I asked.

"I mean all this *memorization* you're doing with your kids. Poetry, history timelines? Math drills? Seriously?" She feigned shock. "You used to be my favorite rebel - my unschooler. This isn't unschooling. You've changed." It was good-natured teasing, very tongue-in-cheek.

I looked at my homeschooling sister, separated by years of curricula, pencils, pens, erasers, workbooks and hours upon hours of discussions. She was my rebel friend - always ready to have difficult conversations, speaking her mind, leaving confused people scratching their heads in her wake. Conversation with her was always a treat.

"Oh, I'm *still* an unschooler," I assured her.

There was some tsk-tsking and laughter. Another friend had joined what by now seemed to turn into an intervention.

I was indignant. "I'm a *classical* unschooler," I affirmed. I raised my glass. I liked the sound of it the moment I said it.

"What?" they both said. "There's no such thing. That doesn't exist."

"Doesn't exist?" I asked, indignant. "Well, it certainly *should!*"

And privately, I thought, "And just in case you're right and it doesn't, I am THE Classical Unschooler."

What is a Classical Education?

A classical education is defined as one characterized by a specific style of learning first originating in Ancient Greece in - you guessed it - the Classical Age. (As an aside, I have a truly great regard for Greeks. Come to think of it, these were people that composed fantastic tales, sailed the seas, made jewelry that surpassed any other at the time it was made and then had the audacity to sit around and try and figure out what the world was made of - they were quite something.) As explained in Plato's dialogue, Classical Education consisted of the trivium and the quadrivium.

Since the chances are high that a homeschooler will be reading this, I feel the need to mention that the trivium, unlike The Terrible Trivium - a demon you meet in the popular read aloud *The Phantom Tollbooth* by Norton Juster - is not malevolent. It is rather the place where three roads of grammar, logic and rhetoric meet. (tri=three, via = roads) More on this later.

Greek children were trained in the trivium before moving on to the quadrivium. The three disciplines in the trivium were grammar, logic and rhetoric and the four subjects the quadrivium dealt with were arithmetic, geometry, music and astronomy. Taken together, the seven were a complete Classical Education in Ancient Greece.

But that was Ancient Greece. As you will see, while I appreciate the structure the classical system of education gives our school day, I also tend to hold on to that structure quite loosely.

Okay, you might say, but that was the Greeks. Why is it relevant? *Is* it relevant?

Well, that depends.

Before I began homeschooling, and indeed, even after we started, it helped me to keep learning about learning, excuse the redundancy. Homeschooling is extremely freeing, but some of us can be terrified with all this newfound freedom, especially when we consider the responsibility that comes with it. Refining my philosophy about what an education is and what it should provide for my children has always been and perhaps will continue to be my concern. As such, I make time to read and write about teaching.

While studying the classical method, my husband and I found it to be true to how we saw our children learning best. We saw the importance of memorization, of a systematic focus on learning the basics first and drilling them until they became second nature. Based on our individual family and our specific convictions, we felt we were very closely aligned with the classical model.

Homeschooling can look different for every family. All this to say that you must decide for yourself where you fall on the big, bad, broad spectrum of homeschooling. This is just one method.

If you would like to know more about classical education beyond my brief introduction to it, should look into Dorothy Sayers' essay **The Lost Tools of Learning**, a quick but worthy read and Susan Wise Bauer's book, **The Well Trained Mind** - pretty much essential reading for anyone thinking of using the Classical Method of education.

The Three Ways or Trivium

Typically, when people speak of being "classical homeschoolers" or "using the classical system of education" it means they believe that learning is best achieved by breaking up the study of the subject they are pursuing into the three stages of grammar, logic and rhetoric. This three level process of training the mind to think is called the trivium. (As mentioned earlier, *tri* in Latin means "three" and *via* means "way" so *trivium* is the place where the three roads of grammar, logic and rhetoric meet.) I will not be dealing with the quadrivium here because we do not use it in our homeschool.

One of the best definitions of "trivium" is by Miriam Joseph in ***The Trivium: The Liberal Arts of Logic, Grammar, and Rhetoric.*** This is how she describes it. "Grammar is the art of inventing symbols and combining them to express thought; logic is the art of thinking; and rhetoric is the art of communicating thought from one mind to another; the adaptation of language to circumstance… Grammar is concerned with the thing as-it-is-symbolized. Logic is concerned with the thing as-it-is-known. Rhetoric is concerned with the thing as-it-is-communicated."

The Grammar Stage

In the grammar stage, the student learns the basic grammar of what he has undertaken, be it music, math, reading or even more complicated pursuits such as building a computer or fixing a car. For instance, the basic grammar of music would be individual notes, and that of reading fluently would be phonograms.

Have you noticed that elementary schools in different parts of the world are still called *grammar* schools, a term that used to be quite familiar here in the United States as well until about the last generation? The assumption at least was that in this stage of their lives, the children would pick up the basic building blocks of the subjects they are being taught. These disparate blocks then would be put together to develop an understanding of how things work and finally to send the student down the path to create or communicate something original, but I am getting ahead of myself.

The thing that is important not to miss here - and one I want to especially emphasize in my argument for classical unschooling - is that the grammar stage is not limited to students of school age.

These are the three stages of learning almost everything at almost every age.

Think of the last time you learned in something completely foreign to you. Chances are, it was broken down to its smallest, most basic elements. You mastered those before you moved on to how they all fit together.

Maybe you taught yourself a new language. In that case, you probably began with tons of names of nouns, pronouns and some verbs. Then you learned to piece them together and finally you got to the point where you could say what you wanted to say in your own words but in a new language.

The word *grammar* comes from Old French *gramaire* or Latin *grammatike*, both of which mean "letters" or "the art of letters."

Any time you are in the information gathering stage, you are learning the grammar of how something works. You are learning what makes it tick from the smallest bits of information you can gather.

The Logic Stage

In the logic stage, the fun begins, well, for me anyway. This is the stage in which the student learns to piece the information together. Consider, for example, that I have recently developed an appreciation of history. I know most of the important events of world history as I have picked them up from textbooks, movies, my own reading, The History Channel, what have you - the wars, the kings, the revolutions and so forth. But then I recently bought a timeline that is so long and detailed that it only fits on the wall of our corridor in our tiny home.

Putting it there, however, brought alive all the history of the world to me.

I now know where these important events that shaped people and cultures fit. Not only do I now have mental pegs of dates and periods where these wars and events fit into the timeline, I also know how they related to each other. I have an understanding of what event led to the other and what was going on in different parts of the world at the same time. I learn, in the logic stage that Marco Polo influenced Christopher Columbus and his journey. I also know that Ancient China was a thriving civilization at the time Marco Polo visited it with his father Niccolo Polo.

Why are these connections important? Because it is connections that help us make sense of the world. But knowledge also has to build on something. Without basic facts connections cannot be made; and simple discrete standalone facts don't teach. Begin with facts and start making connections with other facts and pretty soon, you're learning.

There is some dispute about the origin of the word "logic." It either came from the Old French *logique* or from the Greek word *logos* both of which give us a deeper appreciation of the word as "reason" or "word."

Consider that "grammar" means "letters" and the difference between the two words becomes immediately apparent as progressively more complex: whereas the grammar stage is about letters, the logic stage is about words.

The logic stage in terms of traditional education would roughly coincide with the beginning of middle school. This is when children are able to think in terms of abstract reasoning. Open ended questions become more interesting, because at this stage they have (or are able to easily find out for themselves) the basic blocks of information that fit together - or not.

At this point, in traditional math, they would begin to study algebra. In English, they could reasonably be asked to write a simple (*very* simple) story of their own.

Not unlike the grammar stage, the logic stage also is not limited to students of school age and is the second stage of learning anything. If you were learning to play the guitar, the logic stage would come in when you got comfortable enough playing individual notes, had practiced enough to be able to move your fingers relatively effortlessly over the strings, learned strumming and could move on to playing simple songs. Most of us would think of this stage as the intermediate stage.

The Rhetoric Stage

If grammar = letters and logic = words, then clearly rhetoric must mean sentences, right? Right!

Rhetoric, as we understand it today, especially in the political realm where the word is most used, is language designed to have an impact without any real depth or meaning. But the meaning of rhetoric as it relates to Classical education is actually the exact opposite of the way we use it in the political sense.

Rhetoric is the art of persuasive speaking. It is putting together an argument with the use of well thought out information that has been gathered and digested in the previous two stages.

Traditionally, this is where the student would be able to put together book reports, or write longer stories, participate in debates or at least sufficiently argue with you for an increased allowance in a way that makes you nod in agreement.

To take the example of learning to play the guitar one step farther, you would consider yourself to be in the Rhetoric stage when you could create a tune of your own and play it. You could not have reached this stage before mastering the other two and neither should you expect to do so.

Mastery

Okay, so all that sounds very systematic. The problem is that learning does not proceed from point A to point B in such a systematic manner. These three stages do not progress in a linear fashion nor do they move in a strictly grade-level formation. Just because a student is ten years old does not mean that he is ready to move on to the logic stage and there are plenty of twenty-somethings that are still not able to form coherent arguments.

My posit is that just as learning a new language or a new skill of any sort requires one to pass through the individual stages of training your mind to ascend to the level of mastery, all individual subjects (or skills, if you bristle at the idea of subjects, as I sometimes do) require increasing competence *individually*. This seems obvious - just because you are fluent in Spanish for example, you would not assume that you could then speak Hindi as easily. Or just because a child grasps fractions immediately it does not make him adept at algebra.

Of course, there are overlaps that occur when we break up learning into subjects, but depending on your mental makeup, these overlaps can help or hinder. I mentioned my fascination with history earlier. I tend to learn in a fairly haphazard way - call it natural or intuitive - both sound better than "haphazard." My son tends to do the same. My daughter, however, needs a very methodical, streamlined introduction to every stage or she gets overwhelmed. I don't understand that kind of learning but I respect it. I bend my teaching to it.

And so it is here that I find Sayers' essay that I mentioned earlier (seriously, read it! It will be the best investment in your understanding of classical education ever!) exceptionally perceptive - she reminds us not to think of the trivium as subjects but as *tools*. How well can your child wield each tool, she asks. Once she is adept at using one and is showing signs of moving on, then *and only then* is it time to pick up the next one and not a day before. I would contend that this is to be true regardless of age.

Sayers relates grammar, logic and rhetoric to thinking, arguing and expressing and exhorts teachers to concentrate on
"first forging and learning to handle the tools of learning, using whatever subject [comes] handy as a piece of material on which to doodle until the use of the tool became second nature."

The beauty of the Classical style of education is that the three ways are so different that you won't miss each one when it shows up (Sayers calls them the Poll-parrot, the Pert and the Poetic) but they are also so organic that there is no way around each. Learning does, by its very nature, progress through these three steps on the way to mastery. We are simply guiding our children through these individual steps and providing what they need at every step.

What Is Unschooling?

Unschooling is exactly what it sounds like - at its very core it is the idea that a person can get an education without having to set foot inside a classroom or a school. By extension, unschoolers also take it to mean that the world the child lives and grows up in *is* the classroom, that it provides ample opportunities to learn and grow.

Unschooling is characterized by student-centered, interest-led learning without external compulsions determined by age or grade. Proponents of unschooling claim that when the child is ready to learn something, the internal motivation is usually a much stronger incentive than external rewards and punishments which abound in classrooms and schools.

Unschoolers also maintain that natural curiosity helps children to maintain and strengthen internal motivation to learn rather than instilling in them the desire to wait in boredom or anger until called upon to learn something only because it is now considered the appropriate age by a mandatory committee.

The History of Unschooling

Unschooling began as a movement in the 1970s when John Holt coined the term. Holt was an educator and - like another teacher with the same first name - became disillusioned with the educational system. Instead of considering reform, he began to suggest that people teach their own children. His books *How Children Fail, How Children Learn, Teach Your Own* and *Learning All the Time* amongst others are considered the cornerstones of unschooling. His newsletter *Growing Without Schooling* was the nation's first home education newsletter.

Holt believed that giving children a rich environment was enough training. Children, he said, have a natural curiosity to understand the world around them and would do so anyway if they were not coerced. Schools, he maintained, had failed because they were using the wrong approach to teaching and had instead created people who were afraid of learning because of facing ridicule.

Today, unschooling as a method of learning and as a trend in homeschooling has grown to the point that people are not shocked when the term is spoken and has even enjoyed a certain notoriety amongst societal iconoclasts. (For instance, read this post in Wired: http://www.wired.com/2015/02/silicon-valley-home-schooling/) That you can find articles about unschooling in a mainstream magazine like Outside (http://www.outsideonline.com/1928266/we-dont-need-no-education) speaks volumes about how far unschooling has come.

What Unschooling Is Not

As nebulous as the term is to describe, it is just as hard not to, but I have to be clear in this one regard. When a parent says that she is unschooling her children, she does not mean that she has no regard for their education, as some people believe. In spite of the fact that unschooling is becoming mainstream, there is a thought current that seems to equate unschooling with literally doing nothing to educate the children. This couldn't be farther from the truth. Indeed, a friend of mine who is a teacher claims that even though she went to school she was unschooled the rest of the time. This did not mean that her mother did not care about her education; in fact, just the opposite was true. Her mother cared enough about her that she did not take "school" seriously. My friend had time to decompress, do what she was interested in and - in general - be a child.

It is important also to distinguish between my understanding of unschooling and a certain strain called "radical unschooling." As the name suggests, I believe by embracing unschooling in general and not sending our kids to schools, taking on the complete onus of their education on ourselves, we are considered radical enough. The notion of a radical radical does not appeal to me, if only because I like variety between the adjective and the noun.

Indeed, I would also argue that if you went back to the source and read what Holt had to say about unschooling, it would be closer to just taking a child out of school. At the time Holt was writing, 7Up had just come out and was being advertised as the "un-Cola." John Holt was, I'm quite sure, aware of this marketing prefix and might have adopted it as a nod to the popular culture of the time. At any rate, he related homeschooling to unschooling pretty closely as evidenced by his own footnote in his book *Teach Your Own,* "unschooling: see homeschooling."

Also, unschooling should be distinguished from deschooling.

Deschooling is usually a period of downtime homeschoolers suggest parents should give children after pulling them out of public school. Because public school has its own rhythm and learning on your own with your particular desire and motivation has quite another rhythm, it is a bad idea to jump directly from public school into homeschool. The interim period in which children figuratively do nothing (sleep, play, cook, read) is referred to as deschooling.

    Unschooling, as you can tell, is an ongoing, lifestyle choice whereas deschooling happens for a shorter amount of time.

Some Current Unschooling Writers

Of course I would say (and you have no reason to doubt me, right?) that I think that unschoolers are the most interesting people in the world. They know a ton of stuff, they usually believe in the best their children have to offer, but more than anything else, I love unschoolers because they haven't forgotten that they are still learning as well. Their unschooling philosophy teaches them that learning doesn't happen only in the classroom, that they don't need permission to pick up a skill and that experts don't always have all the right answers. They are unafraid because they are always learning and deeply interested in everything.

Some current writers I would urge you to read if you're considering unschooling are John Taylor Gatto, (He's a behemoth in the homeschooling world, although I don't believe he refers to himself as an unschooler. Just like John Holt, he is a retired public school teacher. If you don't read another book about homeschooling or unschooling, make sure you pick up *Dumbing Us Down* by him) Penelope Trunk, (She blogs often about unschooling and unschools her two sons) Zachary T. Slayback, (his book *The End of School* is excellent!) Peter Gray, Sandra Dodd (but keep in mind she advocates radical unschooling, mentioned earlier). Also be sure to check out Life Learning Magazine. There are tons of other blogs, books and informational articles out there, but don't forget to subscribe to my blog, too.

Enter Classical Unschooling

And here we are. The two forms seem rather extreme. Can ever the twain meet?

The answer is a resounding YES!

Classical Unschooling combines the best of the two supposedly disparate disciplines of Classical education and Unschooling while blending them into a great education not just for your children but for you as well. Since you never stop learning it is easy to incorporate the same tools you use for your children into training your own mind to think and to train yourself.

Train in what? you might ask. And the answer is - anything! I tend to favor reading and learning an adult task for every subject my children are learning at their level, so for instance if they're learning basic arithmetic, you can always read a biography of a famous mathematician (if you're interested in biographies) or the history of how math came to be used or how it got incorporated into the education system as it stands today (if you're interested in history) or why people like or do not like common core math (if you're interested in current affairs) or you can learn algebra and its uses or even calculus (to take a more direct form.)

    The essence of Unschooling is to follow your interest and now that you know *how* to learn and teach best, remember that nothing you learn is ever wasted. I find it hilarious for instance that people say they never use algebra when even finding the cheapest unit cost of one brand of diapers and comparing it against another in the grocery store is algebra.

    Not only does Classical Unschooling put you and your children on a never ending trajectory of learning, it also puts the tools of systematic education at your disposal so that you practice what you preach and model a lifestyle of learning to your children.

The Five Tools of Classical Unschooling

Strewing

One of the biggest takeaways from the philosophy of unschooling is that learning happens everywhere and all the time. The world is your classroom. You do not have to spend hours upon hours at a desk unless it is completely necessary. You do not need an institution dispensing information to you at a specific rate or age level. This is especially true today, where information is ubiquitous and you have only to ask Google or Siri and you carry a GPS system and a calculator everywhere you go.

Unschooling also gives us the term *strewing*. Strewing says that if you want to teach something, you don't need to instruct your students in it as much as get them interested in it. Curiosity and internal motivation takes care of the rest.

Children are especially receptive to strewing in the younger years. Our mornings, for example, are a classic case of strewing. We have lazy mornings and do not begin sit down work until about 10 am. With nothing to do, after breakfast, the children naturally gravitate toward the books that are lying around the living room from the day before or a game that their sibling had played. They distractedly head over to it and, before you know it, have called each other over and picked up a piece of information or two and are interested, involved and learning.

For a more in depth treatment of the subject of strewing and some ideas on how to incorporate it into your day, read my blog post about <u>using strewing as a strategy in Classical education</u>.

Because unschooling only cares about exposure to subjects and not mastery, this is where I differentiate from it. As the parent - and a classically unschooling parent at that - I decide what's important and what's not. The unschooling model gives me the freedom to strew things in my child's path that will interest him and the classical model gives me a system to maximize his understanding of what he is learning.

Strewing gives an easy feel to the homeschool day. I am not held back by institutionalized ideas of grade levels or rigid curriculum. When the child is ready, I can feel free to move him along on to the next level. I am able to do this anywhere and anyhow.

Conversations

One of the most basic features of Classical education was Socratic dialogue. It is also the most basic form of education available to all parents today.

Last year, we bought a new to us minivan. The children began squabbling over who gets to sit where. This was the dialogue that ensued between them and me. The kids are fighting about who gets in the van first. Scrambling, pushing and shoving ensues. Someone gets hurt.
"What happens when you guys get unruly?" I asked.
They stare at me in silence.
"What happened the last time there was fighting and crying about who sits where?"

"You assigned seats," one replies matter-of-factly.

"What's going to happen now, do you think?"

"You'll assign... assign..."

"Order. In other words, I'll make a new rule."

"Oh," they all say at once.

"So what happens when you can't control yourself?"

"Rules are made."

"Yes. Stupid rules. Like assigned seats and who enters when and where and standing in a line with your hands behind your backs."

"Oh."

"So what do you do if you want less rules?"

"Behave ourselves."

"Have self control."

Well, that was easy. The role of government explained in less than five minutes.

    Don't answer questions as much as make them think. Children are curious and they will naturally ask questions. They have a hunger for facts and figures. You do not need to externalize rewards and punishments for much of what you're teaching, although you have the freedom to do that if you want to. That is the power of classical unschooling.

Memorization

Nowhere is the line more firmly drawn in the sand than when it comes to memorization. Unschoolers just cannot see eye to eye with classicals because of this one thing. I say break down that barrier!

Yes, it is possible to look up Google for information, yes, we have amazing tools around us. I, for one, love technology and embrace it (a little too) willingly. But I also love being able to recall the perfect toast during a wedding: "Let me not to the marriage of true minds admit impediments, Love is not love that alters when it alteration finds or bends with the remover to remove." I love being able to know that 12 times 12 is 144 without having to think it through or look it up in my calculator. Poetry, math, history, facts bring as much color to life as art. And being able to improvise is a skill that does not come without a vast reserve of facts at one's disposal.

There is also an argument that claims that creativity cannot flourish without imitation and the emphasis on creativity before being taught the basics of art or writing is putting the cart before the horse.

When you use classical unschooling and memorize the grammar, you give your students mental pegs for life. They now have these mental pegs, this grammar, that they can connect interdisciplinarily and unleash the kind of creativity that they could never reach had they begun with trial and error.

Also, when you begin with grammar, you have the added advantage of having older children teach younger kids as well, integrating learning on multiple levels while also teaching them to teach. Yes, it sounds redundant, but there is an advantage here because you learn better when you teach the subject to someone else. Think about your experience teaching your children and how much more you appreciate what you already know and how much more you understand it now because you've had to break it down into its grammar to teach your children.

The grammar of a thing is a gift.

Cherish it, keep it.

Memorize it.

Interest-led Learning

Okay, be honest, how much of what you learned in school do you remember? Most people can't even find countries on a map. It makes you wonder, doesn't it, what in the world you were doing in school? Classical unschooling gives you the best opportunity to teach children what they *and you* see as the most important skills.

After teaching them to read, write and do basic math (which is not that hard!) why not follow their interests and yours? It's not hard to get children to like what you like. Expose them to your world, expose them to your friends' worlds, take a year off sit-down work and go attend every workshop The Home Depot offers for children, immerse them in the world and see what comes of it.

Follow your interests, follow theirs and if you're worried write down what they learned each day. You would be surprised how much they learn just by being alive. Be curious, be hungry for learning. And not just for your children.

I will add here one thing. I am often asked the question that if your child refuses to learn something you see as important, will you push them to learn it anyway? My answer is always an unequivocal YES! Of course I will. I am their mother. And I will *especially* insist on them learning something if I see talent in a specific field.

So if my son who I really think will have something to do with programming or gaming or computer technology, and refused to do math and coding, yes, I will do whatever is in my power to force, bed, plead, discipline, exhort him into doing it.

It is my job to lead my children to where the dots connect as far as I can see. And I can see much farther than them at this point.

But *for the most part*, I will follow their interests and work with them. I will use their learning styles, teach to their abilities and help them stretch and learn, but I am not abdicating all responsibility. It does not have to be an either-

or case. Classical unschooling works because it can encompass both.

Skills Learning

From the time the children were very little, I included doing chores as part of their school work. This was a precursor to them learning to be comfortable with their hands. Parents sometimes don't like to teach their children chores, partially because it takes longer than doing it yourself. But if you will be spending all day with them, why not use the time to work together as well as play together?

We teach our children to cook, clean and otherwise help out with basic tasks when young with the understanding that as they get older they can learn to do other things on their own. Once I brought home a stationary bicycle that I had my children learn to assemble by looking at the diagrams, with my help.

These are real life skills that become more important as time goes by. Wherever possible, we try to include them in our daily lives. I sometimes bemoan not living on a farm but there's no reason that they can't learn the ins and outs of suburban life. Most of these at a young age involve answering questions but they can become more hands-on.

This model, by the way, could be argued as an unschooling model or an apprenticeship model. One could argue that my daughter is unschooling when she is learning to use the leaf blower to clean the backyard or that my son is under my husband's apprenticeship when he is teaching him to mill grain which will eventually be made into beer.

Why?

Of course, the question that has not been answered is why learn this way? The answer is simple - for a richer life. Who said learning only happens in classrooms? What in the world is a library for? What about a grocery store? What about Google? Go beyond the basic textbooks, open an encyclopedia, go ahead and think. Ask why.

Not only does classical unschooling give your children a deeper, more curious encyclopaedic awareness of the world around them, it deepens your world - your intellectual world, your inner universe. It makes you think, posit, argue with yourself and you will see as you follow this path, that you will begin to get more curious yourself. The world will become more wondrous and filled with awe.

And isn't that the point of it all, anyway?

Classical Unschooling in Action

So far, we have been talking about classical unschooling as theory. Let me give you some insight into what it looks like in our family on a practical basis. You can also check out my blog about out typical day, which changes often, by the way.

If we are going to give children the tools of learning using the steps of grammar, logic and rhetoric, but also have them be interest *and ability* driven, we need some basic subjects to help us along. Many unschoolers tend to be opposed to teaching subjects. I understand that aversion but I also am not completely opposed to subjects as long as the connections between different subjects are made in the right context and the larger picture is shown.

It is normal to want to break a large piece of information into bite-sized pieces to make it more palatable and easy to remember. The problem comes in when history has its own realm and geography has its own and as soon as you begin one, you are to put away the other and the sound of the bell tells you when to do what. The problem is that when there are no interconnections drawn, they remain disparate in the mind of the student. That's not how we tend to learn things in the real world.

For something to be truly grasped, there need to be more connections made in the brain. The more connected an idea is to others, the better it is remembered. The more pegs a concept can hang on, the better its recall and the more creatively it can be used. The more connections are made, the better the recall of any piece of information. (From https://student.societyforscience.org/article/learning-rewires-brain)

 Sayers, in her essay *The Lost Tools of Learning* I spoke of in the last chapter says that we can use the elements of the trivium by applying them to different subjects. In other words, we need subjects as the raw material just as to learn the use of a saw we would need wood.

 The difference between the classical unschooling approach to using subjects and that of traditional school is the margin drawn around each one and between them. Usually, in traditional schools, because the subjects are taught by different teachers, with different styles and sometimes because there are deadlines, tests and other factors involved in the teaching of individual subjects, they never get organically integrated into one whole.

 As a classical unschooler, not only do you have the freedom to cross-reference and integrate learning, it is preferable as a method of teaching and learning. Also, it's plain old more fun.

 Contrary to public school thinking, this is not that hard to achieve. In the home environment where life is lived on a practical basis, unless you impress the school culture on your days artificially, (and there is no need to do so, in my opinion) connections will be made and you can guide your children into making them.

Let me give you an example. Today, we will be covering the three subjects of Bible, history and math. Of course, this means that we've had to work on reading and writing in the past (and still do), using narration, and memorization. The elements of grammar - reading, writing and memorization inform their subject matter. We also take it another step farther by drawing connections between the subjects themselves. This is not hard to do - when studying the timeline, I ask questions that help the children peg their history and Bible into one coherent whole. And while math seems to be a standalone subject, the children care a lot about it when they get paid. Indeed, I was surprised at how quickly they got good at adding quarters, dimes and nickels. The more connections they make, the harder something is to forget.

Speaking of money, I'll also mention that the more they care about something, the easier it becomes to remember and learn as well. Why in the world would the children care to learn anything? Well, because some motivation comes from within. It is part of who they are. Some children are fascinated by trains and planes, some love to cook, others love to read and play video games, even others are more rough and tumble and they need the physical activity of a game to feel fully alive.

It is your job to find out what makes each child unique - chances are you already know - and then to use that as a jumping off point to teach them to learn. Since we already spoke of subjects as raw material, what does it matter what you use as long as they are learning to learn?

Individual Subjects in Classical Unschooling

Let me preface this section by saying that I absolutely hate it when people tell me how to homeschool. So many thoughts come to my head including - but not limited to - smart retorts, sarcasm, wanting to throw the closest object at the person talking and just generalized anger at the whole institution of school that all I can usually do is stare blankly at their teeth as they talk.

So take this - indeed, this section, this entire book - as merely a suggestion. The best thing about homeschooling / unschooling is that *you* are in charge of your children's education. (Incidentally, that's also the worst thing about homeschooling, but that's true of almost everything, isn't it?)

I find it easier (and more reasonable) to stick to the three stages of Grammar, Logic and Rhetoric than follow the public school format of Elementary, Middle and High school. It makes much more sense to give the children the next tool of learning when they have mastered the first tool rather than send them into grade after grade just because they are of a specific age. Sometimes this means hanging back and waiting for them to perfect the use of the same tool over and over and sometimes this includes moving faster than they would in the traditional format of school.

Yes, that means my children never know for sure how to answer when someone asks them what grade they are in. No, I don't care.

So, without further ado, let me tell you how I in a perfect world would and do choose to handle teaching those entrusted to me.

Language Arts

THE GRAMMAR STAGE

At the Grammar stage, I focus extensively on, well, the grammar. This includes teaching reading with phonics and teaching them to write. I have used curriculum to do this, but it is not necessary. I try to go as deep into the grammar as I can without worrying if they will make the connections or not.

It's incredibly hard for me to do - I keep wanting to teach them every detail and to get them to understand to make connections but I try to remind myself that they are not yet at the stage where they can make the connections and even if they don't, it will not affect them *for now*. There's plenty of time to draw connections in the Logic stage. This does not mean that I stop them if they do make these connections. After all, part of the fun of learning is that a-ha moment.

There is no specific age I begin homeschooling. It depends on their readiness level. I have jumped the gun more often than not and always, always regretted it. Not only is it a waste of money to buy curricula and see it thrown around the house (in my case, it was counting bears - I'm sure I can still find some in my couch pillows!) it leads to frustration and self-doubt. If a child is not reading or writing, especially before the age of 7 - 10 it can be anything from a developmental issue to a discipline problem to anything in between. If a parent gets going too early on homeschooling and the child for whatever reason does not "get it," the parent can assume he has failed and give up, or worse, call in unnecessary "experts". It is always a good idea to wait. With my last child, I plan on waiting until he's practically begging to learn to read and write.

I also read to the children quite a bit in this stage. They love anything from picture books to science readers to history readers to long, involved epics. We are almost never without a good audiobook in the car. We each have a well-used library card.

Narration is a great technique to employ in the grammar stage. I mentioned earlier that I absolutely hated being told how to teach my children. I especially loathe it when it comes to the comprehension questions that follow each text. I knew how to crack them like a code in school with no real understanding of the text and I see my daughter trying to do the same thing.

Instead of those comprehension questions that are only there for a teacher who has to deal with a roomful of students, as a classical unschooler, you are much better off asking your children what they understood or remember from the story and relating it or narrating it back to you in their own words. This leads to much better understanding and then you know exactly what they know and can clarify what they understood.

We also memorize. Some would argue that we are not unschoolers because we memorize. I say that's ridiculous. If unschooling is following the children's lead and letting them learn and study what they want to and what they find most pleasurable and memorization is definitely one of those things they enjoy doing, then how is it not part of unschooling? It is not tedious to them and it is not boring. If it doesn't work for your kids, move on, but give it a shot and see if it enhances their world. It might. What do we memorize? Anything from hymns to math tables, to silly songs to poetry, to names of states, capitals, continents, oceans to history timelines.

In the grammar stage of language arts, I pay special attention to writing. One of the things that I struggled with immensely was when to teach writing to my middle child. He is a boy and in typical boy fashion hated writing. He didn't like to sit still. To add to that, he's left-handed. There were some frustrating days.

Now, I knew that boys typically wrote later than girls. This is not a criticism, it's just a fact. I didn't want to create a public school atmosphere at home by pushing him. I didn't want to make him feel stupid because he couldn't do it, so I went easier on him. We did tons of repetition. He did have to practice it everyday. No, we did not use fancy pencils that taught him the right way to grip the pencil. I did ask him to try and write smaller letters, and we did use special paper, but all of a sudden, he began to write normally and well. He surprised me by holding the pen right. And I did teach him writing.

Why do I share this? To tell you that some of this style of homeschooling, especially in the early years, can be fairly amorphous. The idea of children going through an assembly line and learning writing this year and reading that year is a public school construct. Trying to follow that can make you want to tear out your hair. So, don't. Have patience and do it your way.

Neither reading nor writing is natural. I know that unschoolers as a whole don't like to teach their kids to read or write, but I did make efforts to get them to do so. The *desire* to want to read and write might come naturally, but the *act* of it does not, at least, it did not for my children. So I taught them to do both and I emphasized practice. Once they had been taught the tools, they could now be safely left alone to read and write whatever they wanted.

THE LOGIC STAGE

At the Logic stage, the children build on everything they have amassed in the grammar stage. This is an exciting stage, one you know is coming when you see the arguments develop. By that I don't mean bickering, but real arguments. On one blog I read, the writer said he knew his children were ready when they could argue well about why they should get a larger allowance.

At this stage, parents can begin to introduce larger texts to their children and this is the point at which I would feel comfortable letting them answer a few comprehension questions as long as the questions did not ask them to find the right word in the passage and fill in the blanks or offer multiple choice answers. The logic stage is a good time for essay type answers, still in their own words.

I wouldn't stop reading aloud to the children even though they have entered the logic stage. I don't think there is ever a good argument to stop reading aloud. Reading aloud - sharing an imaginative world together - brings a family together as nothing else does. It's not the same as watching a movie. There's a time for that, too, but it's not the same. In our early years of marriage, my husband and I read *The Hitchhiker's Guide to the Galaxy* to each other. I loved it. But I also hated the movie. All the nuance we had been able to communicate to each other from the reading was gone.

For read alouds at the logic stage, it is a good idea to pick books that one can argue about a bit after the reading is done. Fantasy might still appeal to some readers, but that does not mean that it cannot be argued about. Was he right in doing what he did? What should he have done? What are the issues surrounding the situation? (I remember springing the question, "Was Puzzle innocent in agreeing to Shift's plan?" while reading *The Chronicles of Narnia* to my little kids. Needless to say, it didn't get answered very well.) The children may or may not be able to address the questions completely clearly, however, the logic stage is a good time to get the budding logicians develop their argumentative skills.

Memorization and narration is a good skill to carry into the logic stage. Of course, the material will change. For memorization at this stage, I would use famous speeches and monologues from plays rather than poetry and timelines and such. Of course, if there is interest in those, I would continue. This is perhaps also a time the student will be learning a musical instrument. Memorization will continue in the form of learning tunes and practicing music.

For writing, this is a great time for short essays. Some children at this stage are able to put together some pretty good poetry and short stories. Because they are able to see the *connections* between things, they are able to come up with some pretty fantastic tales. They can be discouraged by the fact that their minds move faster than their hands. In that case, I see no problem with typing or writing words for them as they narrate the story to me.

Each individual subject will develop independently, or rather, the tools of learning wielded on math might well be on a different level of mastery than the tools of learning employed on language arts. There is no problem with this. The problem only arises if you begin to think of the individual tools are grades to move the children through.

There is often crossover, so that if the child is at the logic stage in math, she will probably be at the logic stage in language arts, but this is not necessarily true. Writing is one that lags behind for a lot of students. Just gauge where they are and respond to it rather than trying to shove them along.

THE RHETORIC STAGE

The Rhetoric stage is really the point at which they can put forth their own arguments and hold their own by seeing through other arguments, at least partially. And lest you think this sounds incredibly dry, let me also mention that because this is the stage at which most mental pegs are also firmly established and the logic behind them already in place, this is the stage at which metaphor, the special turn of a phrase or the absolute beauty of a monologue will actually be aesthetically pleasing.

This is the stage of Shakespeare, of poetry, of Greek plays as well as of famous speeches.

This is the stage when writing an essay about what matters most to them, about the virtues they hold dear would be most important. As an unschooler, I suggest having the student maybe consider starting a blog for what he or she is passionate about. He will soon develop the means to learn more about it and describe it persuasively. Writing, when you don't care about the subject matter, is dull and boring and an exercise in tedium, but when you care about the matter at hand and are trying to convince someone else to care changes quickly into a matter of art.

    This is also the stage, by the way, in which they are more likely to come up with a business idea or an invention or the plan for a career. Give them all the tools they need (depending on your comfort levels) and let them experiment with it. If they have been solidly grounded in the basics of the earlier two stages, they will be able to figure out if this is a good fit for them. Again, I see no problem in helping them sort things out and always being there not just as a guide but also a strong and involved parent.

Math

THE GRAMMAR STAGE

The grammar stage in math is obvious to a lot of people. Arithmetic, right? Yup. Although there has been some talk of making word problems the beginning of all math, I disagree with this approach. Arithmetic is the most basic building block of all math. Begin with counting and continue into addition, subtraction, multiplication and division.

Here's a caveat, however. Don't try to force a curriculum down your children's throats. What do I mean by that? I mean that many curricula have a specific way of doing things for the craziest reason which is this: *this is how it has always been done.* They use the idea that this is how math has been taught for decades in school classrooms and those kids don't have a problem with it, so if yours does, your kid must be stupid. (I know, I know, they don't come out and say it as such, but the fact that it's on the page and your child doesn't get it is suggestion enough to a lot of homeschoolers.) *Please don't fall for it.* Math is the most logical thing in the world and if your child is not yet at the logic stage in arithmetic, changing the curriculum is not going to help him. Better to focus on the grammar *one more time* and make him memorize it.

I wanted our last math curriculum - no, I will not tell you which one - to burn. And I'm not kidding. (And yes, I have read Fahrenheit 451.) It would not have been enough for me to throw it out in the trash. I needed to see it burn. It was so haphazardly written, with a smattering of this and a smidge of that and followed no logic at all that I was irritated about three months into it. But in an attempt to make the best of what I had, I stuck with it, rearranging it, organizing it, re-organizing it. It did not work.

I'm going to let you in on a shocker. We don't solve word problems. The children *can* solve them, but we are choosing to wait until the logic stage. Why? Because word problems are the *application* of the concepts they are learning in the grammar stage and the application of grammar is called logic. The way most curricula get around this is by teaching the arithmetic of, say, addition and then putting some addition word problems at the bottom. Some others will tell you to look for some words like "in all" or "left" and then figure out how to solve the word problem.

The problem with decoding a word problem is that it's just that - decoding. Applying what you have learned in a word problem is more than decoding the specific term and then *hoping* that the problem makes sense. Hope is not a good strategy in math. Ever. And usually I can tell when my children start to hope that an answer is right. It's when we're moving too fast and they're not getting it. So we go back and over it *one more time*.

I had a friend confide in me that she was never sure of her answers in math in school. She said her strategy for math was hope. How sad is that? I have a feeling it was because of this kind of teaching.

Let me sound like my mother for a minute. Math is the only subject where you can be absolutely sure of the answer, one you can literally argue about and win if you're right. But that certainty only comes from *knowing* your material and not from guessing or "decoding." Tons of material - especially at this stage - focuses on getting you to *understand* the material but then makes the leap into *applying* it and calling it understanding. Of course this makes sense to the parents and so they buy it.

Don't make this mistake.

We have decided to leave word problems alone for now. We intend to leave them alone until I am convinced that the children have mastered the grammar of math and are almost ready for or have entered the logic stage. (If this bothers you or makes you feel like you are waiting too long, at least wait until they are well into their grammar stage by a few years before introducing word problems and not the way most math curricula introduces it.)

Yes, I know this goes against the grain. As I mentioned before, this may not be the way you teach your children. That's okay. This is only one option. For me, I would rather make my children memorize their math facts - there are some excellent resources out there for just such a thing and wait until they are developmentally ready to move on to the next stage.

THE LOGIC STAGE

It is in the logic stage that we tackle word problems and algebra and also geometry. Word problems at this stage will be relatively easy. Algebra and geometry is the application of what has already been covered in the last stage.

Again, I am incredibly frustrated with curricula that introduced concepts of algebra and geometry earlier, that is, before children are ready for them. Just yesterday we came across a perimeter problem along with double digit addition. Look, *I* get it. As an adult, I understand that all you have to do is put the four numbers one on top of the other and add them, but for someone learning the concept of double digit addition in the logic stage, this is not intuitive.

Yes, I know some children do fine with it, but that is not a good enough reason to subject the rest of the students to it. Especially as an unschooler, I find the logic stage incredibly freeing, but as a classical based person, I see the importance of getting a solid basis in the grammar stage so that the logic stage can be more fun and generally fluid.

The logic stage is a good time for field work in math. This is also the time when children are becoming a tiny bit more independent and able to work on their own, so why not make math more practical? Working alongside with you in yard work or landscaping would give them a chance to apply what they have learned and practice it. Application, after all, is the cornerstone of the logic stage.

Include them in any professional or housework that you can see includes math - and trust me - there is a lot of it. I always laugh when people say that they never use algebra but they buy groceries everyday. In a time when most grocery stores no longer put the unit prices of each brand, why not have your children figure out which is the best deal from a lineup? Sewing curtains? Finding out how much fertilizer for your garden? Cooking? Baking? It all uses geometry and / or algebra. Find something that interests them and get them involved - they'll be motivated to learn it.

One last note on the subject - I *do* understand that we have calculators do our work for us, but I also see the importance of memorizing basic math facts. I would not move to the logic stage just because a student "gets it." I can see how a grocery store might be a good place to use a calculator for a quick answer but I prefer my kids to know the answer without a calculator. Yes, we have been known to do math drills and also sing math to memorize it. Memorization is one of the most divisive subjects within the classical and unschooling community. I would search your individual and family beliefs and decide how to proceed in the matter.

THE RHETORIC STAGE

In the rhetoric stage, I would focus math on the real world skills. The rhetoric stage is the perfect stage for growing young adults to focus on honing their skills to enter the professional world. Of course, if you're an unschooler at this point, you've probably already had situations where you have explained finance, but this stage is a good time to get serious about it. Mortgages, debt, economics would be the only thing on the curriculum. I would include budgeting, accounting, daily money management, frugality, debt management - everything I learned in my thirties and was never taught, indeed everything most children do not learn in public schools at all, perhaps never until they are saddled with college debt that they do not understand how they got into in the first place.

The rhetoric stage is a great stage to make sure the concept of money and how it works is introduced and established. There would of course be crossover at this stage from math to literature, economics, philosophy, science and even theology. I wouldn't worry too much about the segues and instead focus on understanding.

Any internships at this stage - even if just with a relative who owns a business - would be invaluable.

This is also the stage when the kids are able to start thinking at least in some seriousness about their professional and financial lives. The idea of interest led learning takes a new intensity and urgency at this stage and it's not a good idea to push the idea of a smattering of this and a smidge of that. Set everything else aside and let the young adult go deeper into whatever area interests him and show how that could be turned into a profession - whether a job or an entrepreneurship. Give him a strong background in math and accounting.

Science

THE GRAMMAR STAGE

The grammar stage of Science is the easiest and the most exciting. For those of us who are terrified of teaching children at home, math and science seem to be the most obvious fears. But the grammar stage of science should be able to take all those out.

Children are naturally curious and this is the least intimidating stage of teaching science, partially because you don't have to "teach" it. You have simply to offer them places and things that would make their learning easier and more interesting. We're unschoolers, remember? I'll get to the classical part in just a bit.

Where do you learn the grammar stage of science? Why, everywhere! The backyard, the patio, the beach, the forest, the hills, the car, the kitchen. Science is everywhere. If you're stumped, just look through some science experiments designed for this age. They are short, quick and usually quite simple and non-messy. You don't need to run out and buy a microscope just yet unless of course *you* are interested in looking through it. (I think this is a great stage to renew your own interest in Science because I remember hating it in school. Really, I mean, what is so exciting about the diagrams in a textbook? Black and white ones at that!) There is much that can be learned about the natural world from simple observation. Now once the children get good at observing, it might be a good idea to buy some field guides to be able to learn to categorize what they are seeing. These field guides can include insects, birds, flowers - whatever strikes your (and their) fancy.

There are two things we tend to do extensively at this stage of science - library books with lots of beautiful pictures and field trips. If I take the children with me to the library, they tend to come back laden with books about animals, birds and insects anyway. It's not something I have to push. Occasionally, I read them biographies of scientists like Louis Pasteur, Madame Curie and others just to cross some disciplinary lines and make it more interesting for me. I don't worry too much at this stage of trying to draw history and science together - that comes soon enough.

As a *classical* unschooler, I do like memorization at this stage. What do we memorize? Pretty much anything that fits into the science box (or not!) and gives the children mental pegs to hang later information on. This could also be highly individualized depending on the student. I know someone who told me that her son had memorized the kinds of spiders that lived in California and when he saw one that was rare, no one except him knew - and he got a new pet that day!

My daughter in particular is almost obsessed with the human body and learning all about it. So I have been very excited to buy her books about the body and have her memorize the names of all the main muscles and bones. My boys tend to be more interested in rocks and soils, so I have them memorize that. Some other options are classes of vertebrates and invertebrates and if you're feeling motivated, you can always check out some of the library books that interest your children, buy some flashcards and record some facts for them to memorize. Keep it simple.

One last point in this stage and that is there will be a bit of an overlap sometimes into geography and history. I said earlier that I don't like to break things up into subjects and this is why. Learning is inherently messy and that's good. Crossing over into a different subject, even in the grammar stage is fine because some memory pegs are interdisciplinary. I don't want to panic or back off just because while learning about soils and rocks for instance my boys have crossed over into geography.

THE RHETORIC STAGE

Of course, all this crossing over interdisciplinary learning is more fun in the logic stage. I have been particularly intrigued by curricula that claims to cross interdisciplinary lines. Dr. Jay Wile's book on studying science through history comes to mind. That is one way of approaching a subject. Of course, I would say that whatever works for you at this stage to make learning more interesting and cover as many memory pegs as you can, do it.

This is the stage at which for a while you might feel like the children are learning nothing because their mind might seem a little jumbled up, but as long as they are getting enough sleep (yes, really, sleep) and are actively engaged in their learning, they will be learning. No, it is not systematic, and it may at times seem haphazard but then one day they will make a brilliant connection with something completely unrelated and you will be flabbergasted.

How do I know this? Because genius - that spark of creativity - that aha moment - doesn't work in a systematic way. Your student already has the basic information he needs. At this stage, he is merely layering the skeletal knowledge he has. He is filling in the gaps, so to speak. So it is okay to flit a little from one area to another.

Einstein in fact encouraged this kind of learning. He called it combinatory play. It was important to him to link seemingly unrelated things in his mind to be able to successfully think. Here's a quote from his notes:

"I soon learned to scent out that which might lead to fundamentals and to turn aside from everything else, from the multitude of things that clutter up the mind and divert it from the essentials."

He writes this as he discovers that the path to understanding the physical world rests on a deeper understanding of math. This is *exactly* what I mean by saying don't worry if your child doesn't seem to follow a systematic way of acquiring information at this stage.

But what if he does? I have one of each kind of learner. I have one who wants to study everything in a straight line with the awareness of where something begins and ends and when we will be done; how many chapters in the book and details of every kind. That's fine, too. The beauty of learning with an unschooling model after all is that it is child-led, so if the student is interested in following a straight path, I see no problem with letting her do so.

Still, I would spend lots of time at the library and get as many books as I could at this stage. And yes, I would pay the fines if I needed to. (Sorry! I know. I hate them, too.) This is not a stage to waste by any means. While exposure and memorization is important at the grammar stage, the logic stage is when much of the information is put together.

This is also a fantastic time for more hands on projects - electronics, crafts and the like.

I would not toss memorization out the door at this point, though. Chances are that if you have built a system of memorizing your children might still want to do so. But at this stage, mnemonics can be used to make memorization easier.

THE RHETORIC STAGE

The rhetoric stage in Science is where things get really interesting. Most high schoolers would be applying the models they learned in the earlier years. So at this stage, there may be some crossover into other subjects because rhetoric is about application. If we remember that rule, this stage should be intriguing because this is the stage where children will develop and test their growing world view and apply it. This is the time they get to ask themselves the big questions, use them, apply them, test them and even argue them in a meaningful way.

Give your students as much room as they need to apply the models and instruction they received in the earlier ages, but also do not be afraid to challenge them. This depends on their personalities, of course. Some students do better at direct instruction and structure whereas some would do better with being left alone to create, search, inquire and study.

At the rhetoric stage of science is where the classical model of dialogue and inquiry will really come into play. Logic would be a good standalone subject at this stage along with whatever field of science the student is pursuing.

This stage is also a good time to have students writing their arguments down or getting them involved in a debate society where they can pursue their models and think things through. Not the least of this is getting them involved in groups where they are able to do this. If peer influence is the largest influence at this time of their lives, we can use that influence to be a good one that challenges them and incites them onto things bigger than themselves - things that matter. This is the way to do it.

History

We have been reading *The Chronicles of Narnia* and it's odd to me to read those passages that reveal how much C.S.Lewis hates the study of history. He mentions it often in the book as boring and "a bunch of dry dates." That has never been the experience of my children. Mention history and they come bounding out of the room cheering that we will be doing something fun. They love history.

Perhaps that is because I love it, too.

THE GRAMMAR STAGE

In the grammar stage of history, we treat it like a story. I love giving the children the sense of the grand flow of history during this stage. They do get a sense of the dates, but I don't require that they understand them.

We spent many a day mentioning the timeline and what B.C. means and what A.D. means and it may have perhaps made sense after the sixth or seventh time, but it didn't matter. Many curricula begin with the idea of explaining the timeline and dates and that ends up as a major stumbling point for many parents with history.

The children are fascinated by the stories - they don't have to understand why exactly the dates go backwards in the BC period and forward in the AD period just yet. If it eases your mind, go ahead and tell them why but it's also okay if that understanding waits until the logic stage.

The grammar stage is the stage of exploration and learning. Take the opportunity to explore history yourself during this time. Don't worry that it doesn't all quite fit in. The fitting in part comes later.

This is a great time to give your children (and yourself, if you're so inclined - I am!) some mental pegs. We memorize a timeline song, so they have an idea of where we are in terms of history when they learn about a civilization. The timeline song includes dates, empires, periods and centuries. This puts the flow of history systematically divided into their heads.

Also remember that children are visual. You can certainly paint a picture with your words, but you can also show them picture books, videos and movies relating to that time period to enhance their learning of it and make history come alive. Coloring books can do the same thing for them. We like to read through the Usborne Book of World History, watch related videos (as I find them) and look at picture books from the library. If I am so inclined, I can also go dig up world maps and find the place we're talking about on it.

This is a good time to include other subjects if you're concerned about compartmentalizing education. There can be a lot of cross referencing between history and other subjects and indeed there is. There is no need to study history in isolation when really all other subjects are deeply intertwined with it. I have a friend - another homeschooling mom - who teaches almost all subjects (except math) using history as a base. She showed me her plan for the year and it was a nice, slim file with chapter numbers.

"What? That's it?" I asked. "What about language arts? What about... oh, yeah." I, with my wanting to pull from multiple sources and places was left speechless by the simplicity of her plan. I saw the beauty in it immediately.

No mention of history is complete without mentioning Susan Wise Bauer. I will say this: I am not a fan of her Story of the World, (I know others that are, but I am not) but I absolutely *love* her books of world history for adults. I would use these as background study reading for you for you, the parent, as you teach your children. Because you now know more, your understanding and therefore your teaching will deepen. (I was also recently introduced to some great writers of the Medieval Age - Joseph & Frances Gies and Lars Brownworth. If the Middle Ages attract you - they do me, it's my favorite historical period, you must read these writers!)

One last caveat - always begin at the beginning of history. You can choose any method you want: the spiral method or the immersion method, but always begin at the beginning. Susan Wise Bauer likes to say that history is essentially a story and if you're not telling it from the beginning, it gets uninteresting pretty quickly.

Perhaps that is what C.S.Lewis' school got wrong about history and now, splattered through all of his literature, we have his distaste of pedantic history.

THE LOGIC STAGE

In the logic stage, we can begin to put all the discrete elements of history together. Children have a much better understanding of dates at this stage and this is the time when other subjects like geography and social studies can integrate into history and make it more interesting. The logic stage is a great time to gauge a child's understanding and interest in history and lead him accordingly to grow in it by introducing science and philosophy or geography as an accompaniment to it.

The logic stage is also a good time to get deeper into the study of history. If you are using a timeline, now would be the time they can learn to craft their own or just study it more often. Because by this time writing and reading is second nature to most children, they can now write little paragraphs about their favorite time period or about a specific item during their time period. Boys, for instance, are instance are always fascinated by the weaponry. Why not have them write and study the catapult and the trebuchet and the Roman times?

Done right, it will be hard to keep history in its box at this stage. The logic stage will force children to go outside the history box and explore science, geography, language, math (yes, math!) and other subjects to get a full understanding of the time. Let them! This is where your unschooling will really shine. Let it!

History is not perfect, by the way, as we all know and much depends on who is doing the narrating. This is the stage in which you would ground your children in the truth, but don't discount something because it is not written perfectly. I'm thinking especially about historical readers which are now available free under the open copyright laws because they've been written so long ago and also things like famous letters and speeches. Sure, they're written from a perspective that is not politically correct. But politically correct textbooks are incredibly boring and suck all the fun out of this stage *and the next*.

Instead, have them read primary sources, have them read interesting things and have lots and lots of conversations. Heritage History is a great company to look into for this. No, they are not paying me for this endorsement. Even if you don't buy their books, the authors unearthed by them give the children something interesting to read during the Logic stage.

One last note about the logic stage - do not discount anything as teaching! History is everywhere. There are historical movies and documentaries, there are graphic novels, even something as simple as jewelry can be a gateway into history, as evidenced by my daughter who pays *very* close attention when jewelry is mentioned and as a result knows the difference between the Minoans and the Mycenaeans. The more *you* read history, the more you will be able to follow along and teach!

THE RHETORIC STAGE

The rhetoric stage of history is when learning comes full circle as some like to put it. The rhetoric stage is when you want to make time to have as many conversations about current events as possible with your student.

But wait, you say, this is about history!

Yes, of course, but a firm grasp of current events requires that the student not only remembers facts, but also that he has made the connections with other subjects and disciplines. This is a great time for her to put out theses, arguments, and make a case for what she thinks should happen in the world.

This stage may or may not coincide with early adulthood or the teenage years and as such can be instrumental in creating the person's worldview and passion. An exciting blend of idealism and fact coupled with a strong awareness of beauty make this a fantastic time to draw them into disciplines like debating and philosophy.

If they're not interested in debate, they might be attracted to theater. Don't miss any opportunity to expose them to good literature, good theater and the arts. Students at the rhetoric stage, whether they admit it or not, have a highly tuned sensitivity to beauty, irony and the poetry of life. It is my belief - you might disagree and that's your prerogative - that as a culture sometimes we don't give our youth enough to care about or do and so they end up disillusioned and cynical. It isn't that they don't care; it's that they can't do anything about it and all this caring makes them seem weak and useless and so they withdraw into themselves.

Give them something to care about, let them do something about it and watch them flourish. Get them involved in places that matter to them. Let them join debate clubs, let them tinker, invent, blog, write, join an internship, get an apprenticeship, volunteer for TED talks, church events. Let them network and meet with people they admire, find out the nitty-gritty of life. They will be enriched by the experience. And so will you!

Geography

THE GRAMMAR STAGE

Geography is one of my other favorite topics related closely to history and I suspect it might be my son's favorite as well. In the grammar stage of geography, our mental pegs include names, names, names. Yes, some of these are hard to pronounce, especially for little children, especially *my* little children, but with enough practice, repetition and memorization, they get it.

Sometimes, we memorize with songs set to music. There are lots of resources for geography facts set to music. You just have to look. Audio Memory is a company that comes to mind. I believe it is one of the oldest and most established. If you go this route, make sure it's music that will not irritate *you*. I was looking for an audio accompaniment to math facts once and I found something that was inexpensive. I was so glad I previewed it, though because the math facts were set to rap! Nothing against those of you who like rap, but I find it unpalatable and the idea of playing it in my car so that the children could learn math was so distasteful that it was just not going to happen. So I found a different one that sang math facts to classical music.

    Anyway, back to geography. In the grammar stage, we memorize names of continents, countries, oceans, capitals, states, state capitals. We also memorize and learn about atmospheric phenomena - clouds and rain and hail and thunder. We take care to talk about how these occur. We also memorize and learn about types of clouds, layers of the atmosphere, layers of the earth's crust. By the way, if you want your children to memorize geography facts but don't know where to begin, feel free to open any book for about their age range and keep a stack of cue cards ready. As soon as you come across a fact, write it down. This is how I created a list of things I wanted them to know. Of course, you can always buy these facts, but I like searching them out.

THE LOGIC STAGE

The logic stage in geography is a great time to take field trips and explore life through Google maps and other such websites that give you the sense of being there. It is not always possible to travel (although that would be my top priority.) Let the children draw their own connections at this stage. They will naturally be interdisciplinary and you will have a hard time separating geography from science, from math and clearly from language arts. It doesn't matter. This is the fun part of learning. If you have done the hard work of establishing the groundwork in the grammar stage, this stage becomes one more of putting things together and "aha moments" abound.

Stamp collecting is a great hobby at this time of the geography stage. Many times, stamps have pictures on them that are commemorative of times and events in history and can lead to fascinating discussions that cover government, ethics, economics and the like. Do not get in a hurry to leap over these conversations or avoid them. These conversations are the lifeblood of unschooling. I have often said to my children, "I don't know. We can find out." And they have just as often replied, "Ask Google!" So even if you have to do some research in the area, this is a great way to get into geography and learn it in the most haphazard but fun way possible.

You might find yourself drawn into this area more yourself. If you are taking the advice to travel, you will also see much of what you have learned in your past come alive. You might be inclined to pick up books and learn more about things that seemed not to interest you in the past. Don't panic. This is all very normal and the best part about classical unschooling.

THE RHETORIC STAGE

In the rhetoric stage of classical unschooling, students can learn to give back to their community and to the world in general. It could provide an opportunity to travel as well as a way for them to feel deeply connected to the world around them, not to mention develop an understanding of human beings as only such endeavors would.

Included in the rhetoric stage of geography would be mission work, community work, helping a nonprofit, interning, helping old or disabled relatives or neighbors. These are invaluable experiences, especially at a time when it is imperative to relate places to people.

Of course, not everything has to be travel related. News stories about current events around the world can be incredibly educational too and a great pathway into finding out more and relating these to other subjects. Integration is the heart of the rhetoric stage.

Other languages

Let me say this before I begin: I do not teach Latin. Nope. Not going to happen. Yes, I've heard the arguments for it. Yes, I see the value in it for those that are interested. No, I will not teach it. I tend to be quite practical in the matter of education and lean a little more to the unschooling side than the classical side of things here. But here I stand. I cannot do otherwise.

I might be more inclined to teach my children a practical language they can speak. Because I grew up in India, I am fluent in two languages besides English and I am considering teaching them to speak Hindi. We are at the very basic beginning stages of it, but because I haven't spoken it in a while, I would need some brushing up as well.

If my children show an interest in wanting to pick up another language, teaching it would also depend on why it is they want to learn it. If they just have a passing interest in it, I would offer apps such as a Duolingo or Memorize and get them started. If it grows far beyond that, I would consider getting them into a class that preferably immerses them in it. (There is a time and place for classes outside of school of course! I do however prefer that my children are older when they attend a class to get the full benefit of it.)

If you speak a specific language, the advantage of teaching it to your children is that you can converse with them in it. Immersion is central to learning to speak a language. As such, I will not be following a rigorous curriculum for it but watching movies and speaking it around them for them enough for them to pick it up.

Music and Other

Music is a language unto its own and I could have included it in the previous section, but I wanted to give it its own space and include it into other things that might interest the child. I firmly believe that music and athleticism is not something you can push on a child. I mean, you can, and with consistent, good training, you might even help produce something like a good music player or someone who plays a sport well, but for it to mean something to the individual you are raising, I would wait to see intrinsic motivation in this regard.

Of course, since we're unschoolers, we can introduce them to various things and gauge interest and talent.

I was quite surprised, for instance, when I saw the budding of musical talent in my daughter. We were at a museum and while I was quite miffed that they had set up a *"classroom"* to teach *homeschoolers* the basics of music, my daughter volunteered to go to the front of the class and play a relatively complicated rhythm that she made up on the spur of the moment. That was when I knew that she had not just the inclination and ability to learn music but also a keen interest in doing so. We started small - a homeschool co-op and then more advanced lessons.

    You are around your children all day long. Unless you are avoiding them, you know what they love to do, what they are naturally attracted to and where their abilities lie. My son, for instance, *might* be interested in the piano but we're waiting to find out. For now, he seems drawn to sounding out words (a natural representation of a mind that takes pleasure in seeing patterns and how things fit together) finding out how things work and playing video games. My other son is more rough and tumble. I can see him playing sports, but it would be a disaster if I pushed our middle son into it. Watch your children and send them in the direction of their own strengths and talents. Then watch them blossom.

Education is a Conversation, Not a Performance

Back when I was about five years old, I would come home from my private school, go to the play blackboard that my parents had bought me and teach my imaginary classroom. I loved reliving the day at school as the teacher, not the student. All I knew of teaching was standing in front of a blackboard and talking to a bunch of kids.

When I began homeschooling, I had no such assumptions, thank God! I had been privileged to have the time to read books and get an idea what I believed to be right about education. Of course, after we started homeschooling, those ideas themselves changed and were perfected, *are being changed and perfected* every single day.

That's because teaching cannot be a performance if it is done right.

There is no script. You have a goal, but there a thousand ways to get there. And those thousand ways will be different depending on your personality, your spouse's personality, each of your children's personalities and your specific family dynamic.

You are not on stage. Your children are not an audience. Some days, you're all in the peanut gallery together. Remember that. And appreciate it. And, more importantly, enjoy it.

(And come back and read my blog. I'd like to keep *our* conversation going.)

Updates Along the Journey

It has been a good three years since I first wrote this book and a lot has changed since then. The children have grown and are continuing to grow in spite of my exhortations to stop.

What has not changed is the basic template we use in our homeschool, which has been laid out here. I find it much easier to modify something rather than create something new from scratch. Also, I find it incredibly hard *not* to modify something. That is because I firmly believe that homeschooling is and must be individualized to your family, your style and what works for you.

If you're interested in creating your own homeschooling curriculum, I have written a separate book to guide you along that journey. Look for it on Amazon under the title *Create Your Own Homeschooling Curriculum: A Step by Step Guide.*

Acknowledgments

I am so very grateful to my blog readers who encourage me to keep writing and all the homeschoolers I have met over the years - whatever their style of teaching may be. I have learned so much from all of you and continue to learn. I hope your enthusiasm for educating your children and yourselves and your passion for sharing the wisdom you have gathered never wanes.

I am thankful also to my parents - and especially my mother - who though weren't able to homeschool me ingrained in me some basic solid principles of learning that have not left me.

Thank you to my children who know me to be a very flawed teacher but love me anyway and to my husband, James, who both grounds me and gives me wings.

And, of course, I owe a huge debt of gratitude that will never be fulfilled to Christ, who daily guides me.

Thank you.

About the Author

Purva Brown is a writer & homeschooling mother of three children. Her work has appeared in *Practical Homeschooling Magazine, Kidaround Magazine* amongst other places. Her writing was also included in *Highway 99: A Literary Journey Through California's Central Valley.*

She blogs at TheClassicalUnschooler.com

Copyright © 2016 Purva Brown

All rights reserved.

No parts of this publication may be reproduced, stored in a retrieval system, or transmitted in any form or by any means, electronic, mechanical, photocopying, recording, or otherwise, without the prior written permission of the copyright owner.

Under no circumstances may any part of this book be copied for resale.

Made in the USA
Middletown, DE
19 March 2021